D0789149

DEC 1 5

FACT? FICTION?

FACT OR FICTION?

The Tuskegee Airmen

Tammy Gagne

Mitchell Lane
PUBLISHERS
P.O. Box 196
Hockessin, DE 19707
www.mitchelllane.com

Mitchell Lane
PUBLISHERS

Printing   1   2   3   4   5   6   7   8

Audie Murphy
Buffalo Bill Cody
The Buffalo Soldiers
Eliot Ness

Francis Marion
Robin Hood
The Tuskegee Airmen
Wyatt Earp

Library of Congress Cataloging-in-Publication Data
Gagne, Tammy.
 Tuskegee airmen / by Tammy Gagne.
     pages cm. — (Fact or fiction?)
 Includes bibliographical references and index.
 Audience: Grades 3-6.
 ISBN 978-1-61228-966-3 (library bound)
 1. World War, 1939–1945—Participation, African American—Juvenile literature.
2. United States. Army Air Forces. Fighter Squadron, 99th—History—Juvenile literature. 3. African American air pilots—History—Juvenile literature. 4. World War, 1939–1945—Aerial operations, American—Juvenile literature. 5. Tuskegee Army Air Field (Ala.)—Juvenile literature. 6. World War, 1939–1945—Campaigns—Western Front—Juvenile literature. 7. World War, 1939–1945—Regimental histories—United States—Juvenile literature. I. Title.
 D810.N4G34 2015
 940.54'4973—dc23
                                                                                              2015003186

eBook ISBN: 978-1-61228-967-0

                                                                                                          PBP

CONTENTS

Chapter 1
Pioneering Pilots 5

Chapter 2
Based on a True Story 9

Chapter 3
Taking a Stand 13

Chapter 4
Making it to the Big Screen 19

Chapter 5
Never, Not Ever? 23

Fact or Fiction? 26
Chapter Notes 28
Glossary 30
Works Consulted 31
Further Reading 31
On the Internet 31
Index 32

Words in **bold** throughout can be found in the Glossary.

The Tuskegee Airmen played an important role in World War II. The African-American fighter pilots saw their share of action overseas.

CHAPTER 1

Pioneering Pilots

"As I was pulling out, a German fighter was on my tail, so I made a steep turn, and just as I turned, another enemy plane shot across my nose. I fired and fired and fired until he went into a steep dive and crashed."[1] This sounds like something one teenager might say to another after playing a video game. But these words were actually spoken by American World War II fighter pilot Robert Williams.

Lasting from 1939 until 1945, World War II was the most devastating war the world had ever seen. The United States was a member of the Allies, which also included Great Britain, Canada, and France. Led by Adolf Hitler, Germany was part of the Axis forces along with Italy and Japan. Hitler's Nazi movement targeted Jewish people. He blamed the Jews for Germany losing World War I. He also thought that Germans were superior to the Jews in every way. He wanted to banish Jews from society completely. Millions of Jews perished in what is known as the Holocaust.

The senseless idea that one group of people is better than another is called **prejudice**. The Allies wanted to put an end to Hitler's horrible treatment of the Jewish people. But while the war was being fought in Europe, another battle was raging on in the United States. As part of the Allied Forces, the US was fighting a war involving great prejudice—Hitler's inhumane treatment of the Jews. But many of these same Americans held their own prejudice—against African Americans.

Tens of thousands of Americans flew aircraft in World War II. These brave young men risked their lives by serving their country. And they were greatly admired for their courage and their piloting skills. But many white Americans did not want blacks to become pilots. Rumors claimed that blacks were less capable of learning how to fly than whites.

A group of servicemen would crush those racist rumors. A project created by the United States Army Air Corps in 1941 at Alabama's Tuskegee Institute (now Tuskegee University) trained nearly a thousand African Americans as fighter pilots, and many others as ground crewmen servicing the planes. Called the Tuskegee Airmen, the all-black group was credited with 15,500 **sorties** (individual missions) during the war. Their primary mission was escorting American bombers deep into enemy territory. Journalist Burt Folkart wrote, "They destroyed 260 enemy planes, damaged 148 others and sank a Nazi destroyer. No US bomber was shot down while flying under the protection of the fighter group."[2]

The Tuskegee Airmen earned 150 Distinguished Flying Crosses. According to the US Air Force, these medals are awarded to fliers who "have distinguished [themselves] in actual combat in support of operations by heroism or extraordinary achievement while participating in an aerial flight."[3] One of the recipients was Robert Williams. As a member of the 332nd Fighter Group, he flew fifty missions.

The wartime efforts of the Tuskegee Airmen were just the beginning for many of these intelligent, driven men. Following the war, a number of them became doctors, lawyers, and judges—professions largely unavailable to most African Americans of the time period. Other former Tuskegee Airmen became politicians and community leaders. Many also continued the fight for civil rights—seeking equality for all citizens, no matter what their skin color.

But even after everything the Tuskegee Airmen accomplished, many Americans still had no idea who they were. Williams wanted to change that. He spent many years trying to convince someone to make a film about the trailblazing pilots—and the discrimination they faced. "He never lost his enthusiasm for the project," the *Bangor Daily News* reported, "approaching almost every major studio and TV station."[4]

Williams said that he found the general lack of knowledge about the Tuskegee Airmen as devastating as the racism the group endured. "It's never been part of American history," he explained. "There's nothing in the books about it."[5]

It would take several decades before he succeeded in getting the story told. Finally, in 1995, HBO released the film *The Tuskegee Airmen*. It won three Emmy Awards, a Peabody, a Cable Ace Award, and two NAACP Image Awards. One of the movie's main characters, played by Laurence Fishburne, was based on Robert Williams.

Tuskegee Airman Charles A. Anderson took First Lady Eleanor Roosevelt for a ride in his airplane in 1941.

CHAPTER 2

Based on a True Story

T*he Tuskegee Airmen* offered a great deal of factual information about the pilots. But the film also included some fiction. The writers created the characters from the details of different Tuskegee Airmen's lives. Both the real Robert Williams and the fictional Hannibal Lee, for example, were from Ottumwa, Iowa. Both men rose to the rank of captain and received the Distinguished Flying Cross. But according to Williams's 1997 **obituary**, the character of Lee was only "loosely based on Williams."[1]

The real-life Williams experienced little racism in his early life. Growing up in Iowa, Williams had attended **integrated** schools which welcomed both black and white students. But that would change when he traveled to Alabama. The Tuskegee training facilities were **segregated**, meaning that blacks and whites were kept separate. "One of the pluses of the integrated experience was that I never learned to hate white people and I never learned to hold them in awe," he said. "I knew at an early age that they were no different from me intellectually or any other way. The differences between us were only the paint job."[2]

In the film, one of Hannibal Lee's proudest moments comes when First Lady Eleanor Roosevelt visits the flight school shortly after its formation and asks him to take her for a ride in his plane. Surprisingly, this scene was not made up by the writers. It actually took place. But it was not Williams who took her for the now-famous ride.

According to the Franklin D. Roosevelt Presidential Library and Museum, "In 1941 [Mrs. Roosevelt] visited Tuskegee Army Air Field and asked to take a flight with one of the Tuskegee pilots. Although the Secret Service was anxious about the ride, flight instructor Charles A. Anderson piloted Mrs. Roosevelt over the skies of Alabama for over an hour. That flight proved for Mrs. Roosevelt that blacks could fly airplanes and she did everything in her power to help them in that endeavor. Mrs. Roosevelt marked the occasion with a photograph of herself and Mr. Anderson which she promptly brought back to her husband, the President of the United States, and successfully urged FDR to utilize the 99th Squadron in combat missions."[3]

While Hannibal Lee did not exist, Benjamin Davis, Jr. did. As a lieutenant colonel, he commanded the 99th Fighter Squadron. The film version of Davis had much in common with the actual airman. In one scene, Davis tells his pilots that he attended West Point, the US Military Academy in New York. He tells them that none of the white cadets spoke to him during the four years he was there.

Shortly after the film's release, the Los Angeles Sentinel reported that the real Davis "endured four years of the 'silent treatment' at West Point. His strength of spirit and determination allowed him to overcome this unfair treatment and graduate with honors. He later became the first Three Star African American general in the military."[4]

The film focuses on the 99th Fighter Squadron, the first African-American fighter squadron. This unit was eventually joined by three other squadrons—the 100th, the 301st, and the 302nd—to become the 332nd Fighter Group. Steve Jones of *USA Today* reviewed the movie when it became available on Blu-ray in 2012. Although he was describing the film's characters, his words hold true for what the real Tuskegee Airmen endured as well. "They are given plenty of reason to quit: having to move to a colored-only train car when they first arrive in the South; instructors intent on seeing them fail; inferior equipment; and lack of respect from white pilots," he wrote. "But they have even more compelling reasons to **persevere**: They embody the hopes and dreams of their race, and they find satisfaction in succeeding in the face of adversity and proving the haters wrong."[5]

At first many white pilots didn't want the African Americans in Italy. But as the Tuskegee Airmen proved their worth, the bomber crews–who were white–changed their minds. It was clear that the 332nd Squadron was the best at protecting the bombers from marauding German fighter planes. The *Los Angeles Sentinel* reported, "Throughout the entire mission history of the 332nd, no bomber they were ever assigned to was lost to enemy fire."[6]

When President Barack Obama was inaugurated in 2009, many of the surviving Tuskegee Airmen were in their 80s and 90s. Still, 170 of them made the trip to Washington, DC, to witness the historic event.

CHAPTER 3

Taking a Stand

Journalist Brenda Payton writes a regular column in the *Oakland Tribune*. In more than twenty-five years with the paper, she has tackled many important social issues such as racism. She has won numerous awards for her work. In 2014, Payton wrote about someone else who made enormous progress in the fight for racial equality—her own father. "My dad, James B. Williams, was a Tuskegee Airman,"[1] she stated proudly. What most people know about the Tuskegee Airmen, they have learned from reading books or watching movies about the group. But Payton got to learn about this important part of history from someone who had experienced it firsthand.

She began her column by pointing out, "I said he was a Tuskegee Airman. The truth is he is and always will be a Tuskegee Airman. I think for most of them, it was a defining period in their lives."[2]

Payton continued, "My dad was an engineering officer and his part of the story unfolded at Freeman Field in Indiana. In April 1945, he and 100 other Tuskegee Airmen refused to sign a document establishing a whites-only officers club. Refusing a direct order in wartime could be considered treason and punishable by death. He told his commanding officer simply, 'If I can't go into the officers club, then I shouldn't be an officer.'"[3]

The men were definitely not rewarded for their actions—at least not for many years. Instead, they were taken to another base and placed under house arrest. According to Payton, the men "faced a charge of treason, punishable by death."[4] Most of the men, including Williams, were released within a few days. But a letter about the incident was added to each of their files. It stated that "they were a disgrace to their country and their race."[5]

"Growing up, I remember my father talking about the letter of **reprimand**," recalled Payton. "My brother and I didn't realize the seriousness of what he'd faced. We knew he didn't think the reprimand was legitimate. Still, it was in his file."[6] It would stay there until 1995, the same year *The Tuskegee Airmen* was released. That year, at the convention of the Tuskegee Airmen, it was officially removed. Twelve years later the men received the Congressional Gold Medal. They were finally being honored as heroes.

When President Barack Obama was **inaugurated** in 2009, James Williams and his fellow Tuskegee Airmen were invited to the ceremony. Payton went with her father to the historic event. "When Obama took the oath of office," she remembered, "Section 15 of the West Front of the Capitol, where the Tuskegee Airmen were seated, didn't erupt in cheers and applause. They seemed more like they were holding their breath, waiting to make sure it was really

President George W. Bush awards the Congressional Gold Medal to Tuskegee Airmen for their bravery.

happening. About 170 of the surviving members, now in their 80s and 90s, endured the travel, the crowds, the cold, to stand witness to one of the most significant moments in American history."[7]

A much younger Williams had been relentless in his own fight against prejudice. But even after all that he and his fellow Tuskegee Airmen had accomplished, he was surprised by how far his nation had come. And he was more than willing to share the credit. "I never thought I would see that [a black president]," he admitted. "I'm thrilled. I'm glad to see the country has

In 1948, President Harry Truman eliminated segregation from the United States armed forces. The bold move made many newspaper headlines.

grown up to the point it could accept that. I give a lot of credit to the young whites who were very enthusiastic about him. He couldn't have done it without them."[8]

Williams and his fellow pilots helped open doors for generations of African Americans interested in serving their country. In 1948, President Harry Truman issued Executive Order 9981: "It is hereby declared to be the policy of the President that there shall be equality of treatment and opportunity for all persons in the armed services without regard to race, color, religion or national origin."[9] Historians now call the protest in Indiana the Freeman Field Mutiny. Many insist that the event played a key role in Truman's order desegregating the United States military.

EXECUTIVE ORDER

ESTABLISHING THE PRESIDENT'S COMMITTEE ON EQUALITY OF TREATMENT AND OPPORTUNITY IN THE ARMED SERVICES

WHEREAS it is essential that there be maintained in the armed services of the United States the highest standards of democracy, with equality of treatment and opportunity for all those who serve in our country's defense:

NOW, THEREFORE, by virtue of the authority vested in me as President of the United States, by the Constitution and the statutes of the United States, and as Commander in Chief of the armed services, it is hereby ordered as follows:

1. It is hereby declared to be the policy of the President that there shall be equality of treatment and opportunity for all persons in the armed services without regard to race, color, religion or national origin. This policy shall be put into effect as rapidly as possible, having due regard to the time required to effectuate any necessary changes without impairing efficiency or morale.

2. There shall be created in the National Military Establishment an advisory committee to be known as the President's Committee on Equality of Treatment and Opportunity in the Armed Services, which shall be composed of seven members to be designated by the President.

3. The Committee is authorized on behalf of the President to examine into the rules, procedures and practices of the armed services in order to determine in what respect such rules, procedures and practices may be altered or improved with a view to carrying out the policy of this order. The Committee shall confer and advise with the Secretary of Defense, the Secretary

Executive Order 9981, issued by President Harry Truman, brought racial equality to the United States armed forces.

*A second film about the Tuskegee Airmen, called **Red Tails**, appeared in theaters in 2012.*

CHAPTER 4

Making it to the Big Screen

I n 2012 another film about the Tuskegee Airmen was released. It was called *Red Tails*, after the red color the real airmen applied to the tail assemblies of their planes. "We got the reddest paint we could find and painted our aircraft," said Herbert Carter, a member of the 99th Fighter Squadron. "We wanted the bomber crews to know when we were escorting them and we wanted to make sure the [enemy] knew when we were airborne and in their territory."[1]

Unlike the HBO movie, *Red Tails* would make it all the way to the big screen. George Lucas, the famous director of the *Star Wars* movies, had wanted to turn the Tuskegee Airmen story into a major motion picture for many years. But he quickly found out that producing this film wasn't going to be a simple task.

A 2004 PBS documentary about the 332nd Fighter Group had been named *The Tuskegee Airmen: They Fought Two Wars*. This title refers to the dual struggles the African-American pilots faced—World War II itself, and the racism of the people who tried to keep them out of the air. Now it seemed that there was a new battle on the horizon. It had to do with race. It also had to do with money.

Lucas approached several major Hollywood studios about the project. None was interested. "It's because it's an all-Black movie," Lucas explained. "There are no major White roles in it at all. I showed it to [the major studio executives] and they said, 'No. We don't know how to market a movie like this.' It's one of the first all-Black action films ever made."[2]

Lucas eventually decided to finance the movie himself. He spent $58 million of his own money on the film. "It was a project that I instantly was attracted to and was determined to get made,"[3] he said.

Despite Hollywood's worries, *Red Tails* was a hit at the box office. Musician and actor Ne-Yo played pilot Andrew "Smokey" Salem in the film. When the movie was ranked number two in box office receipts after its opening weekend, Ne-Yo told MTV, "I feel like we definitely did what we set out to do, which was make sure these incredible men, the Tuskegee Airmen, got the recognition that they deserved for the incredible things that they did for this country."[4] He also added that through the film they were able to prove to Hollywood that an all-black cast could fill movie theater seats.

Many film **critics** weren't as kind as the audiences, though. The Rotten Tomatoes film rating website only gave it a 40 percent mark, though noted reviewer Roger Ebert praised the film for its action scenes. "The scenes of aerial combat are skillfully done and exciting. It makes the point that the airmen were skilled and courageous, and played a historic role in the eventual integration of our armed services."[5]

But Ebert insisted the movie could have done more than that. "Years ago, my father had a friend who flew bombers over Germany," the critic continued. "He spoke of the immediate reality that each mission could very likely be the last. Here, I didn't feel fear as the pilots took off. They had pride, patriotism and zeal, yes, but their hands must have been sweating and their guts must have been churning. I would have appreciated their thoughtful late-night conversations about the meaning of it all."[6]

Ebert stated that HBO's *The Tuskegee Airmen* was more fact-based than *Red Tails*. He also pointed out, "The only character of general rank in the cast of 'Red Tails' is [the fictional] Gen. Luntz, played by Gerald McRaney, one of the few white actors in the film."[7]

Lucas has never been one to be discouraged by critics. He said, "I have only one **agenda**, and that's for a lot of young people to see this movie. I think kids who see this, be they black or white, will walk out thinking these [Airmen] were cool."[8]

The movie's director, Anthony Hemingway, said that as a black man and artist, he felt a responsibility to tell this story. "I'm glad we can change awareness with this movie. But ultimately, to me *Red Tails* isn't just a black story, it's an American success story."[9]

The Tuskegee Airmen came from all over the United States. Edward C. Gleed, seen here in front of a P-51 fighter plane named "Creamer's Dream," was from Lawrence, Kansas.

Never, Not Ever?

The Tuskegee Airmen accomplished many things both during and after World War II. But what sometimes gets questioned is the claim that they never lost a bomber to enemy fire. This claim has been referred to as a *fact* countless times since the end of the war. Speeches, books, and newspaper articles—not to mention many class projects—have included this impressive tidbit. It even appears at the end of *The Tuskegee Airmen* film along with photos of the real-life pilots. But is it actually true?

Daniel Haulman has worked at the Air Force Historical Research Agency since 1982. William Holton is a historian with the Tuskegee Airmen, Inc. In 2006, *Los Angeles Times* journalist Jenny Jarvie reported that the two men had "uncovered combat mission reports that showed that at least a few bombers escorted by the airmen were shot down by German planes."[1]

Haulman and Holton insisted that they simply wanted to make sure the history was recorded properly. "If I didn't share my knowledge, I would be **derelict** in my duties as historian of the Tuskegee Airmen," Holton explained. "Of course, this is painful.

Some of the people I admire very much are **incensed**."[2]

One of those incensed people was retired Colonel Richard Macon, a former Tuskegee Airman. "I think this is being initiated by people who want to discredit the fact that we were unique,"[3] he said.

His fellow pilot, Carroll Woods, agreed. "I think they are trying to destroy our record. What's the point now?" Woods went as far as calling the new findings "outrageous."[4]

Shortly after Haulman and Holton made their announcement, white World War II bomber pilot Warren Ludlum came forward to support the new claims. He reported being shot down by enemy planes in 1944 while being escorted by the Tuskegee Airmen. He pointed out that he was taken to a prisoner-of-war camp he shared with one of the African Americans, Starling Penn.

Alan L. Gropman, a professor at the National Defense University in Washington, DC, wrote *The Air Force Integrates: 1945-1964.* Gropman stresses that Ludlum's information falls short of disproving the Tuskegee Airmen's record. "The fact the two men were in the same prisoner-of-war camp does not necessarily mean the Tuskegee Airmen were escorting those particular airplanes,"[5] he stated.

Benjamin Davis, Jr. wrote about the Tuskegee Airmen's perfect record in his 1991 autobiography. He stated that General Yantis "Buck" Taylor, commander of the 306th Fighter Wing, of which the 332nd Fighter Group was a part, had given him a letter that "remarked that ours was a fine military organization: Among our accomplishments, we had achieved the distinction of never losing a single bomber to enemy fighters on an escort mission."[6]

But Haulman's research led him to other documents that disputed the claim. One such document was the 1944 order awarding Davis the Distinguished Flying Cross. It praised him for "so skillfully disposing his squadrons that in spite of the large number of enemy fighters, the bomber formation suffered only a few losses."[7]

Whether the Tuskegee Airmen never lost a bomber or suffered only a few losses, the fact remains that these men were among the best pilots in the history of the US Air Force. Part of the problem for many people is the language that's used to state the facts.

"By calling it a myth," Gropman explained, "they are saying the men have been lying, the whole organization has been lying. It seems like the men were deliberately promoting this falsehood. They weren't. They believed in it earnestly."[8]

He added, "Even if they lost three or four bombers, it would still be minuscule compared to the losses incurred by white pilots who also escorted bombers."[9]

"Despite the dispute," wrote Jenny Jarvie of the *Los Angeles Times*, "the historians, airmen and others agree that the group's legacy rests not on whether they lost any bombers but on the broader role they served."[10] The Tuskegee Airmen changed the way the entire world thought about African Americans and their unquestionable abilities.

FACT OR FICTION?

The Tuskegee Airmen have become legends of American history. Like many other legends, though, their story has become a mix of fact and fiction. Let's examine some of the biggest differences between what is historical fact and what is fiction.

FICTION:　The Tuskegee Airmen were inferior to white pilots. A report in September 1943 said that the 99th Fighter Squadron was not effective in combat and should be removed.

FACT:　An exhaustive study indicated that the 99th had performed as well as all-white squadrons.

FICTION:　The Tuskegee Airmen never lost a bomber to enemy action.

FACT:　This is covered in detail in Chapter 5.

FICTION:　The Tuskegee Airmen sank a Nazi destroyer.

FACT:　The Tuskegee Airmen attacked a former Italian destroyer that had been converted by the Germans to a torpedo boat, so technically it wasn't a destroyer. More to the point, the vessel was heavily damaged and put out of action, but it did not sink.

FICTION:　Because white officers didn't want any Tuskegee Airmen to become aces (pilots who shot down at least five enemy aircraft), they changed the records of pilot Lee Archer to show that he only downed four German planes.

FACT:　Documents show that Archer claimed only four victories, and he was given credit for all of them. There is no evidence that Tuskegee claims were treated any differently than whites.

FICTION: The Tuskegee Airmen's accomplishments ended when World War II was over.

FACT: A number of Tuskegee Airmen remained in military service and served in Korea and Vietnam. Three became generals. One of them, Daniel James Jr., faced down then-Libyan dictator Muammar el-Qaddafi in 1970. Qaddafi wanted an American base in Libya to close down. With several armored vehicles behind him, Qaddafi confronted James. In what sounds like something from the Wild West, James said, "He had a fancy gun and a holster and kept his hand on it. I had my .45 [caliber pistol] in my belt. I told him to move his hand away. If he had pulled that gun, he never would have cleared his holster."[1] Qaddafi backed down.

FICTION: Because the Tuskegee Airmen were so effective in protecting bombers, many bomber crews specifically asked for them as escorts. Benjamin Davis even put the nickname "By Request" on the side of his plane.

FACT: There were more than 20 different bomber groups and seven fighter groups. As Daniel Haulman of the Air Force Historical Research Agency observes, "To say that the 332d Fighter Group did a better job at escorting bombers than any of the other fighter groups is very difficult to prove from an examination of the World War II documents . . . . Because the assignments [to escort bombers] were made on a rotational basis by headquarters, apparently without discrimination, the idea that bombardment crews could request one fighter group over another for escort duty, and get it, is not likely."[2]

CONCLUSION: "Whoever dispenses with the myths that have come to circulate around the Tuskegee Airmen in the many decades since World War II emerges with a greater appreciation for what they actually accomplished," says Haulman. "The Tuskegee Airmen proved that they were equal to the other fighter pilots with whom they served heroically during World War II. Their exemplary performance opened the door for the racial integration of the military services, beginning with the Air Force, and contributed ultimately to the end of racial segregation in the United States."[3]

Chapter 1: Pioneering Pilots

1. John B. Holway, *Red Tails: An Oral History of the Tuskegee Airmen* (Mineola, NY: Dover Publications, 2011), p. 255.
2. Burt Folkart, "Robert Williams; Flier Helped Tell Story of Tuskegee Airmen." *Los Angeles Times*, September 11, 1997. http://articles.latimes.com/1997/sep/11/local/me-31221
3. "Distinguished Flying Cross," *Air Force Personnel Center*. http://www.afpc.af.mil/library/factsheets/factsheet.asp?id=7767
4. "Movie shows hardships faced by airmen." Bangor Daily News, August 23, 1995. http://news.google.com/newspapers?nid=2457&dat=19950823&id=EqdJAAAAIBAJ&sjid=Bw4NAAAAIBAJ&pg=4921,2037994
5. Ibid.

Chapter 2: Based on a True Story

1. Burt Folkart, "Robert Williams; Flier Helped Tell Story of Tuskegee Airmen." *Los Angeles Times*, September 11, 1997. http://articles.latimes.com/1997/sep/11/local/me-31221
2. "Movie shows hardships faced by airmen." *Bangor Daily News*, August 23, 1995. http://news.google.com/newspapers?nid=2457&dat=19950823&id=EbqdJAAAAIBAJ&sjid=Bw4NAAAAIBAJ&pg=4921,2037994
3. "The Tuskegee Airmen and Eleanor Roosevelt." Franklin D. Roosevelt Presidential Library and Museum. http://docs.fdrlibrary.marist.edu/tuskegee.html
4. "The Tuskegee Airmen Make Triumphant Return on HBO." *Los Angeles Sentinel*, August 23, 1995.
5. Steve Jones, "DVD Extra: 'The Tuskegee Airmen.'" *USA Today*, January 20, 2012. http://usatoday30.usatoday.com/life/story/2012-01-19/tuskegee-airmen-dvd-extra/52683878/1
6. "Tuskegee Airmen Make Triumphant Return."

Chapter 3: Taking a Stand

1. Brenda Payton, "Thinking of Tuskegee Airman father during Black History Month." *Oakland Tribune*, February 22, 2014. http://www.contracostatimes.com/news/ci_25207264/payton-thinking-tuskegee-airman-father-during-black-history
2. Ibid.
3. Ibid.
4. Brenda Payton, "Tuskegee Airman James Williams at inauguration." *San Francisco Gate*, January 25, 2009. http://www.sfgate.com/opinion/article/Tuskegee-Airman-James-Williams-at-inauguration-3174750.php
5. Ibid.
6. Payton, "Father."
7. Payton, "James Williams."
8. Ibid.
9. Truman Library, Executive Order 9981.
10. http://www.trumanlibrary.org/9981a.htm

Chapter 4: Making it to the Big Screen

1. "The First Black Pilots in the American Military: Red Tails, The Tuskegee Airmen in World War II." *For Love of Liberty—The Story of America's Black Patriots.* http://forloveofliberty.org/overview/Tuskegee_Airmen.html
2. "Hollywood Refused to Fund 'Red Tails' Because of All-Black Cast, Lucas Says." *Afro-American Red Star*, January 28, 2012.
3. Marco R. della Cava, "Lucas flies solo with 'Red Tails.'" Gannett News Service, January 4, 2012.
4. Rob Markman, "'Red Tails' Proves All-Black Cast Can Soar At Box Office. MTV.com, January 26, 2012. http://www.mtv.com/news/articles/1678007/ne-yo-red-tails-box-office.jhtml
5. Roger Ebert, "Red Tails." RogerEbert.com, January 18, 2012. http://www.rogerebert.com/reviews/red-tails-2012
6. Ibid.
7. Ibid.
8. della Cava, "Lucas flies solo."
9. Ibid.

Chapter 5: Never, Not Ever?

1. Jennie Jarvie, "Setting the record straight on the Tuskegee Airmen." *Los Angeles Times*, December 24, 2006. http://articles.latimes.com/2006/dec/24/nation/na-tuskegee24
2. Ibid.
3. Ibid.
4. "Records Said to Dispute Tuskegee Airmen Lore." Associated Press, December 11, 2006. http://www.nbcnews.com/id/16158108/ns/us_news-life/t/records-said-dispute-tuskegee-airmen-lore/#.U06rf2fD92s
5. Jarvie, "Setting the record straight."
6. Ibid.
7. Ibid.
8. Ibid.
9. "Records Said to Dispute Tuskegee Airmen Lore."
10. Jarvie, "Setting the record straight."

Tuskegee Airmen—Fact and Fiction

1. "The Tuskegee Airmen: 5 Fascinating Facts." History.com, January 20, 2012. http://www.history.com/news/the-tuskegee-airmen-5-fascinating-facts
2. Daniel Haulman, "Nine Myths about the Tuskegee Airmen." Tuskegee University, October 21, 2011. http://www.tuskegee.edu
3. Ibid.

agenda (uh-JEN-duh)—a motive for doing something

critic (KRIT-ik)—a person who makes or gives a judgment of the value, worth, beauty, or excellence of something

derelict (DAIR-uh-likt)—neglectful of one's duty

inaugurate (in-AW-gyuh-rate)—to take office with suitable ceremonies

incense (in-SENSS)—to make very angry

integrate (IN-tuh-grate)—to bring people of different races together in a social group or institution, such as a school

obituary (oh-BICH-oo-ehr-ee)—a notice of a person's death (as in a newspaper)

persevere (pur-suh-VEER)—to keep at something in spite of difficulties, opposition, or discouragement

prejudice (PREJ-uh-dis)—preconceived opinion not based on fact

reprimand (REP-ruh-mand)—a severe or formal criticism

segregate (SEG-ruh-gate)—to separate by race

sortie (sohr-TEE)—a mission conducted by an aircraft

WORKS CONSULTED

della Cava, Marco R. "Lucas flies solo with 'Red Tails.'" Gannett News Service, January 4, 2012.

Ebert, Roger. "Red Tails." RogerEbert.com, January 18, 2012. http://www.rogerebert.com/reviews/red-tails-2012

"The First Black Pilots in the American Military: Red Tails, The Tuskegee Airmen in World War II." *For Love of Liberty—The Story of America's Black Patriots.* http://forloveofliberty.org/overview/Tuskegee_Airmen.html

Folkart, Burt. "Robert Williams; Flier Helped Tell Story of Tuskegee Airmen." *Los Angeles Times*, September 11, 1997. http://articles.latimes.com/1997/sep/11/local/me-31221

Hardesty, Von. *Black Wings: Courageous Stories of African Americans in Aviation and Space History.* New York: HarperCollins, 2008.

Haulman, Daniel. "Nine Myths about the Tuskegee Airmen." Tuskegee University, October 21, 2011. http://www.tuskegee.edu

"Hollywood Refused to Fund 'Red Tails' Because of All-Black Cast, Lucas Says." *Afro-American Red Star*, January 28, 2012.

Holway, John B. *Red Tails: An Oral History of the Tuskegee Airmen.* Mineola, NY: Dover Publications, Inc., 2011.

Jarvie, Jennie. "Setting the record straight on the Tuskegee Airmen." *Los Angeles Times*, December 24, 2006. http://articles.latimes.com/2006/dec/24/nation/na-tuskegee24

Jones, Steve. "DVD Extra: 'The Tuskegee Airmen.'" *USA Today*, January 20, 2012. http://usatoday30.usatoday.com/life/story/2012-01-19/tuskegee-airmen-dvd-extra/52683878/1

Markman, Rob. "'Red Tails' Proves All-Black Cast Can Soar At Box Office." MTV.com, January 26, 2012. http://www.mtv.com/news/articles/1678007/ne-yo-red-tails-box-office.jhtml

"Movie shows hardships faced by airmen." *Bangor Daily News*, August 23, 1995. http://news.google.com/newspapers?nid=2457&dat=19950823&id=EqdJAAAAIBAJ&sjid=Bw4NAAAAIBAJ&pg=4921,2037994

Payton, Brenda. "Thinking of Tuskegee Airman father during Black History Month." *Oakland Tribune*, February 22, 2014. http://www.contracostatimes.com/news/ci_25207264/payton-thinking-tuskegee-airman-father-during-black-history

Payton, Brenda. "Tuskegee Airman James Williams at inauguration." *San Francisco Gate*, January 25, 2009. http://www.sfgate.com/opinion/article/Tuskegee-Airman-James-Williams-at-inauguration-3174750.php

"Records Said to Dispute Tuskegee Airmen Lore." Associated Press, December 11, 2006. http://www.nbcnews.com/id/16158108/ns/us_news-life/t/records-said-dispute-tuskegee-airmen-lore/#.U06rf2fD92s

Red Tails. LucasFilm Ltd., 2012.

The Tuskegee Airmen. HBO Pictures, 1995.

Tuskegee Airmen. History.com. http://www.history.com/topics/world-war-ii/tuskegee-airmen

"The Tuskegee Airmen: 5 Fascinating Facts." History.com, January 20, 2012. http://www.history.com/news/the-tuskegee-airmen-5-fascinating-facts

"The Tuskegee Airmen and Eleanor Roosevelt." Franklin D. Roosevelt Presidential Library and Museum. http://docs.fdrlibrary.marist.edu/tuskegee.html

"The Tuskegee Airmen Make Triumphant Return on HBO." *Los Angeles Sentinel*, August 23, 1995.

FURTHER READING

Burgan, Michael. *World War II Pilots: An Interactive History Adventure*. North Mankato, MN: Capstone Press, 2013.

De Capua, Sarah E. *The Tuskegee Airmen: Journey to Freedom*. Chanhassen, MN: The Child's World, 2004.

Earl, Sari. *Benjamin O. Davis, Jr.: Air Force General & Tuskegee Airmen Leader*. North Mankato, MN: ABDO, 2010.

Roop, Peter and Connie Roop. *Tales of Famous Heroes*. New York: Scholastic, 2010.

ON THE INTERNET

National Park Service, Tuskegee Airmen. http://www.nps.gov/tuai/index.htm

Tuskegee Airmen Inc. http://tuskegeeairmen.org/

The Tuskegee Airmen National Historic Museum. http://tuskegeeairmennationalmuseum.org/

99th Fighter Squadron   10-11, 19
100th Fighter Squadron   11
301st Fighter Squadron   11
302nd Fighter Squadron   11
332nd Fighter Group   7, 11, 19
Allies   5
Anderson, Charles A.   8, 10
Archer, Lee   26
Axis Forces   5
Brown, Roscoe   15
Bush, President George W.   15
Carter, Herbert   19
Congressional Gold Medal   14-15
civil rights   7
Davis, Benjamin O.   10, 24, 26-27
Distinguished Flying Cross   6, 9, 27
Ebert, Roger   20-21
Executive Order 9981   16-17
Fishburne, Laurence   7
Freeman Field Mutiny   17
Gleed, Edward C.   24
Haulman, Daniel   25-27
Hemingway, Anthony   21
Hitler, Adolf   5-6
Holton, William   25-26

James, Daniel Jr.   27
Lucas, George   19-21
Ludlum, Warren   26
Macon, Richard   26
Nazis   5-6
Ne-Yo   20
Obama, President Barack   12, 14
Penn, Starling   24
racism   5-6, 15
red paint   19
Red Tails (film)   18-21
Roosevelt, Eleanor   8, 10
segregation   9, 17
Taylor, Yantis "Buck"   24
Truman, President Harry   16-17
The Tuskegee Airmen (film)   21, 25
The Tuskegee Airmen: They Fought Two Wars (PBS documentary)   19
Tuskegee University   6
West Point   10-11
Williams, James B.   13
Williams, Robert   5-7, 9
Woods, Carroll   26
World War I   5
World War II   5-6, 19, 25-26

ABOUT THE AUTHOR

Tammy Gagne is the author of numerous books for adults and children, including *Eliot Ness* and *Robin Hood* for Mitchell Lane Publishers. She resides in northern New England with her husband and son. One of her favorite pastimes is visiting schools to speak to kids about the writing process.